LISTFUL
THINKING

List Out Your Life

STERLING CHILDREN'S BOOKS
New York

STERLING CHILDREN'S BOOKS
New York

An Imprint of Sterling Publishing Co., Inc.
1166 Avenue of the Americas
New York, NY 10036

ISBN 978-1-4549-3219-2

Distributed in Canada by Sterling Publishing Co., Inc.
c/o Canadian Manda Group, 664 Annette Street
Toronto, Ontario M6S 2C8, Canada
Distributed in the United Kingdom by GMC Distribution Services
Castle Place, 166 High Street, Lewes, East Sussex BN7 1XU, England
Distributed in Australia by NewSouth Books
45 Beach Street, Coogee, NSW 2034, Australia

For information about custom editions, special sales, and premium and corporate purchases,
please contact Sterling Special Sales at 800-805-5489 or specialsales@sterlingpublishing.com.

Manufactured in Canada

Lot #:
2 4 6 8 10 9 7 5 3 1
09/18

sterlingpublishing.com

Text by Chloe Gordon

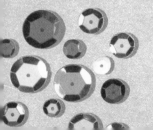

LET'S FACE IT—YOU'RE A SUPER-SPECIAL HUMAN BEING.

Why? Because nobody else shares your glow.

You're **65** percent water and **35** percent opinions, daydreams, and aspirations. If somebody looked inside you, they'd find all that glitter, curiosity, and quintessential essence of **YOU** just sloshing around. This little book of lists is your chance to celebrate yourself and what makes you sparkle! These lists will help you invent, remember, and chronicle the oodles of magical you. Use your imagination, your zest, and your breathtaking originality to explore what tickles your fancy. Whether you're listing all the crazy things you'll be when you grow up or designing your dream home, this book is the place to get it all out!

Fill these lists with spectacular inventions, ingenious plans, heartwarming memories, and cozy secrets.

☀ LET ALL THAT **YOU** SHINE. ☀

And most of all—be proud of who you are and who you'll be!

Smells and tastes can bring back all sorts of cozy,
nostalgic memories. What are some of your favorite foods?

_____

_____

_____

_____

_____

_____

_____

_____

_____

_____

_____

_____

_____

_____

_____

_____

_____

_____

From aliens to ghosts to telekinesis,
what supernatural phenomena do you believe in?

You're opening up your own theme park, just for YOU!
List everything you'll include, from cotton candy stands
to fortune tellers to massive roller coasters.

_____

_____

_____

_____

_____

_____

_____

_____

_____

_____

_____

_____

_____

_____

_____

_____

_____

_____

Sometimes the place where you grow up can feel small, but it's home.
List some of your favorite things about your hometown.

From tuba to fiddle to melodica, list all
the instruments you'd love to jam out on.

From pillow fights to bumper-car rides to rainbow
grilled cheese sandwiches, list how you'd enjoy a perfect day.

_____

_____

_____

_____

_____

_____

_____

_____

_____

_____

_____

_____

_____

HELLO
my name is
_____

_____

_____

Imagine you could invent a bubble gum that tasted like anything you wanted. What flavors would you create?

_____

_____

_____

_____

_____

_____

_____

_____

_____

_____

_____

_____

_____

_____

_____

_____

_____

Maybe you LOVE rubbing puppy tummies and get queasy holding a slug from your garden. Rate stuff you've touched, from sublime to horrid.

_____

_____

_____

_____

_____

_____

_____

_____

_____

_____

_____

_____

_____

_____

_____

_____

_____

_____

_____

_____

List all the tropical fruits you can think of in 30 seconds!

From finger-painting to pep talks to braiding hair,
list stuff you know you're good at.

_____

_____

_____

_____

_____

_____

_____

_____

_____

_____

_____

_____

_____

_____

_____

_____

_____

_____

Maybe you appreciate your mom's strength or your best friend's
ability to make people giggle. Whom do you admire and why?

_____

_____

_____

_____

_____

_____

_____

_____

_____

_____

_____

_____

_____

_____

_____

_____

From rose gardens to strip malls,
list all the places you've been in your dreams.

Chocolate cake, mango lassi, peanut butter cookies . . .
list your most favorite sweets.

Everybody knows rock stars have all sorts of special stuff in their dressing rooms. From sparkling water from the Piedmont region of Italy to organic coconut oil foot massages, what extravagant things would you insist on backstage?

Fresh flowers, gasoline, bacon . . .
list your favorite smells.

_____

_____

_____

_____

_____

_____

_____

_____

_____

_____

_____

_____

_____

_____

_____

_____

_____

_____

From pie-baker to investment banker to physicist, the world is at your fingertips. Write down the jobs you'd love to have someday.

Somebody special is having a birthday—and you're throwing them the best surprise party ever! From piñatas to ice cream cake to pin-the-tail-on-the-unicorn, list how you're going to celebrate.

It's a gorgeous snowy day outside. What are some of your favorite activities to do in this frosty wonderland?

_____

_____

_____

_____

_____

_____

_____

_____

_____

_____

_____

_____

_____

_____

_____

_____

List some zany pet names to bestow on your
future furry (or feathered) friends.

Everybody knows taco Tuesdays are the best.
Rate school lunches from yum to yuck.

_____
_____
_____
_____
_____
_____
_____
_____
_____
_____
_____
_____
_____
_____
_____
_____
_____
_____
_____
_____

Your memories are special because you're the only person who has them.
List your most meaningful memories—happy, sad, or bittersweet.

_____

_____

_____

_____

_____

_____

_____

_____

_____

_____

_____

_____

_____

_____

_____

HELLO
my name is

Snails in butter, dried crickets, squid ink pasta . . .
what are some foods you'd never EVER try? (A few years from
now you can look back and see if you've changed your mind!)

_____

_____

_____

_____

_____

_____

_____

_____

_____

_____

_____

_____

_____

_____

_____

_____

_____

_____

Think about your best friend. Maybe it's Violet from softball or your pet hamster, Gooby. List some words you would use to describe them and why they're special.

_____

_____

_____

_____

_____

_____

_____

_____

_____

_____

_____

_____

_____

_____

_____

_____

_____

You've been hired as a DJ at your local radio station. This is your chance to create the perfect playlist showcasing your impeccable taste. List the songs you'd want to share with the world.

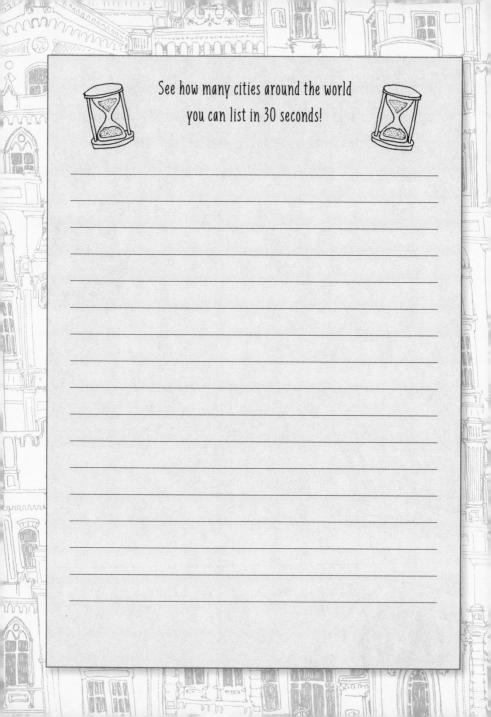

See how many cities around the world
you can list in 30 seconds!

Maybe you would never wear shoes,
or maybe you really want to have a full-on food fight.
What would you do if there were no more rules?

_____

_____

_____

_____

_____

_____

_____

_____

_____

_____

_____

_____

_____

_____

_____

_____

_____

_____

Whether you're an incredible athlete, dedicated fan, or somebody who doesn't consider sports their thing, there are lots of ways to exercise. What are some of your favorites?

_____

_____

_____

_____

_____

_____

_____

_____

_____

_____

_____

_____

_____

_____

_____

_____

_____

_____

_____

From designing awesome sneakers to fronting a
powerhouse rock band, list all the things you'd be
famous for if you were a celebrity.

_____

_____

_____

_____

_____

_____

_____

_____

_____

_____

_____

_____

_____

_____

_____

_____

You can always count on your friends. What are some of the nicest things they've done for you?

You have great friends because YOU'RE a good friend, too.
How do you show your friends you care?

_____

_____

_____

_____

_____

_____

_____

_____

_____

_____

_____

_____

_____

_____

_____

_____

Everyone knows that veggies are yummy and healthy. What are some of your favorites, and how do you like to eat them? Do you roast them in the oven, sauté them on the stovetop, or dunk them in dips?

_____

_____

_____

_____

_____

_____

_____

_____

_____

_____

_____

_____

_____

_____

_____

_____

_____

What are some ways that you pamper yourself?
Do you take a bubble bath or have a favorite meal? List them!

Maybe you love fruit-scented erasers,
glittery folders, or rainbow markers.
List all the school supplies you can't live without.

Art imitates life. Who are some characters from TV, books, and movies that remind you of yourself?

Make a list of spells you'd most like to be able to use,
from charms that help you ace quizzes to hexes that
make your enemies quack like ducks.

Kittens, babies, emojis ... rate supposedly adorable
things from squee-worthy to barf-inducing.

_____

_____

_____

_____

_____

_____

_____

_____

_____

_____

_____

_____

_____

_____

_____

_____

_____

_____

From the jungles of South America to the tropical waters of Hawaii,
list all the places around the world you'd like to visit.

What are some of your biggest secrets?
List them here at your own peril!

_____
_____
_____
_____
_____
_____
_____
_____
_____
_____
_____
_____
_____
_____
_____
_____
_____
_____
_____
_____
_____
_____

Who inspires you? Think of artists, activists, celebrities, or even people you encounter every day. Write their names down and explain why you look up to them.

_____

_____

_____

_____

_____

_____

_____

_____

_____

_____

_____

_____

_____

_____

_____

_____

_____

_____

_____

_____

Some are impressive tongue twisters, while others
sound straight-up silly. List your favorite words!

_____
_____
_____
_____
_____
_____
_____
_____
_____
_____
_____
_____
_____
_____
_____
_____
_____
_____

You're finally a homeowner! From a rooftop pool
to a giant room full of trampolines, list all the crazy things
you'd want in your fantasy house.

_____

_____

_____

_____

_____

_____

_____

_____

_____

_____

_____

_____

_____

_____

_____

You've built your dream house—now where are you going to put it?
From Mars to the bottom of the ocean to a desert oasis,
list all the extraordinary places you'd love to reside.

What do you like to do in spring? Do you plant seeds
or use binoculars to watch the birds come back?
List your favorite springtime activities.

_____

_____

_____

_____

_____

_____

_____

_____

_____

_____

_____

_____

_____

_____

_____

_____

List as many burger toppings as
you can in 30 seconds!

_____

_____

_____

_____

_____

_____

_____

_____

_____

_____

_____

_____

_____

_____

_____

_____

_____

_____

From hoverboards to deep-sea submarines, rank the
different ways you can get around from holy moly to meh.

_____

_____

_____

_____

_____

_____

_____

_____

_____

_____

_____

_____

_____

_____

_____

_____

_____

_____

_____

Your dream job is going great and you've just been given a
penthouse office in the city of your dreams! From a lazy river
to a milkshake bar, how do you deck out your space?

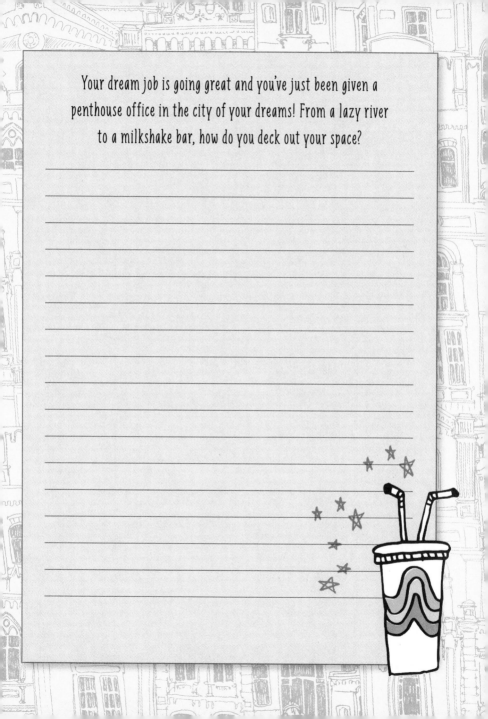

What are the best books you've ever read? Leave a little
note reminding yourself why they've meant so much to you.

Cats, pizza, hanging out with pals—what makes you happiest?
List the greatest joys in your life.

_____

_____

_____

_____

_____

_____

_____

_____

_____

_____

_____

_____

_____

_____

_____

_____

_____

_____

Sometimes you just want to eat junk.
What are some of your favorite junk food snacks?

List your favorite people in the world. If you want,
you can write a memory beside each name to remind
yourself why they matter to you.

_____

_____

_____

_____

_____

_____

_____

_____

_____

_____

_____

_____

_____

_____

_____

_____

_____

_____

_____

Macaroni, linguini, penne . . .
list all your favorite pastas.

_____

_____

_____

_____

_____

_____

_____

_____

_____

_____

_____

_____

_____

_____

_____

_____

_____

_____

From marzipan to long division to your baby sister,
list things you thought you would HATE but actually adore.

_____

_____

_____

_____

_____

_____

_____

_____

_____

_____

_____

_____

_____

_____

_____

_____

Perhaps you dream of world peace or
the end of global warming.
List your hopes for our planet.

Maybe you're volunteering at a local soup kitchen or raising money
to support a cause you believe in. Brainstorm some ways you
can give back to your community.

_____

_____

_____

_____

_____

_____

_____

_____

_____

_____

_____

_____

_____

_____

_____

_____

_____

_____

_____

Movies make us laugh, cry, and see things differently.
List your favorites.

_____

_____

_____

_____

_____

_____

_____

_____

_____

_____

_____

_____

_____

_____

_____

_____

As the next mad genius of your generation, you've discovered a way to create tons of hybrid animal species. List all the animals you'd love to hatch in your secret lab, from fish-dogs to horse-birds!

?!

Think about the people and animals that you consider family and list them below.

_____

_____

_____

_____

_____

_____

_____

_____

_____

_____

_____

_____

_____

_____

_____

_____

_____

_____

Maybe your toes are shaped like French fries,
or you've got a funny freckle.
List all your favorite parts of your body.

_____

_____

_____

_____

_____

_____

_____

_____

_____

_____

_____

_____

_____

_____

_____

_____

_____

_____

You're designing your own line of gorgeous nail polish!
List alluring colors and names.

List as many famous animals, fictional
or real, as you can in 30 seconds!

_____

_____

_____

_____

_____

_____

_____

_____

_____

_____

_____

_____

_____

_____

Some you're laughing with, others you're laughing at.
List comedians and "funny" TV shows or
movies from hilarious to NOT.

_____

_____

_____

_____

_____

_____

_____

_____

_____

_____

_____

_____

_____

_____

_____

_____

_____

_____

_____

_____

Humans are lucky to share this planet with all sorts of
incredible creatures. From tiny fish to huge gorillas,
list some of your favorite animals.

_____

_____

_____

_____

_____

_____

_____

_____

_____

_____

_____

_____

_____

_____

_____

_____

_____

Autumn is great for crunching leaves and heading back to class. What do you love the most about fall?

_____

_____

_____

_____

_____

_____

_____

_____

_____

_____

_____

_____

_____

_____

_____

_____

_____

You can belt them out in the shower or blast them in the car.
List your favorite songs of all time.

Being afraid is the first step toward being brave.
What are some things you'd love to get up
the nerve to try someday?

_____

_____

_____

_____

_____

_____

_____

_____

_____

_____

_____

_____

_____

_____

_____

_____

Fruits are sweet and refreshing—just like you!
List your favorites and how you like to eat them. Do you dunk
banana in peanut butter? Or freeze your grapes for a cool dessert?

_____

_____

_____

_____

_____

_____

_____

_____

_____

_____

_____

_____

_____

_____

_____

_____

_____

_____

_____

_____

Remember that time you burnt your homemade lemon pie?
Or the shot you missed at your last basketball game?
What are some skills you want to work to get better at?

_____

_____

_____

_____

_____

_____

_____

_____

_____

_____

_____

_____

_____

_____

_____

_____

_____

_____

From frying pans designed to help you cook the perfect egg to subway systems connecting massive cities, lots of tools have been invented to make life easier. What are some inventions you wish existed?

_____

_____

_____

_____

_____

_____

_____

_____

_____

_____

_____

_____

_____

_____

_____

_____

_____

_____

Maybe you've got a truckload of sass or a big scoop of zest!
When things get rough, how do you get tough?

_____

_____

_____

_____

_____

_____

_____

_____

_____

_____

_____

_____

_____

_____

_____

_____

_____

If you could meet anyone who ever lived, who would it be?
Make a list of all the people you'd travel
through time and space to meet.

List all the different types of cheese
you can in 30 seconds!

_____

_____

_____

_____

_____

_____

_____

_____

_____

_____

_____

_____

_____

_____

_____

_____

_____

_____

_____

From butt wiggles to karate kicks,
list your go-to dance moves.

You're starting a farm! Maybe you'll stick to veggies like corn and beets or you'll introduce some cute dairy cows and woolly sheep into the mix. What will you plant and nurture?

_____

_____

_____

_____

_____

_____

_____

_____

_____

_____

_____

_____

_____

_____

_____

_____

_____

_____

_____

Someday soon you're going to fall in love.
From a contagious laugh to super-smarts,
what are some things you want in your future beau?

_____

_____

_____

_____

_____

_____

_____

_____

_____

_____

_____

_____

_____

_____

_____

_____

_____

_____

_____

_____

_____

Yeah, you're helpful, but sometimes you'd rather just lounge around on the sofa. List the chores your parents make you do from bearable to blech.

_____

_____

_____

_____

_____

_____

_____

_____

_____

_____

_____

_____

_____

_____

_____

_____

_____

_____

Write a list of all the things you'd do if
you were invisible for a day.

Make a list of all the crazy costumes you've worn for
Halloweens of the past, from awesome to cringe-worthy.

_____

_____

_____

_____

_____

_____

_____

_____

_____

_____

_____

_____

_____

_____

_____

_____

_____

List all the nutty Halloween costumes
you hope to wear in the future!

_____

_____

_____

_____

_____

_____

_____

_____

_____

_____

_____

_____

_____

_____

_____

_____

_____

Maybe it's your fuzzy slippers or your strawberry toothpaste.
List your favorite self-care essentials.

Make a list of silly inside jokes you have with your friends, family, and even yourself.

_____

_____

_____

_____

_____

_____

_____

_____

_____

_____

_____

_____

_____

_____

_____

_____

_____

_____

_____

_____

List as many crunchy snacks
as you can in 30 seconds!

_____

_____

_____

_____

_____

_____

_____

_____

_____

_____

_____

_____

_____

_____

_____

_____

_____

_____

Perhaps it's the quilt your grandma knit or your
stuffed octopus. List your most precious possessions.

_____

_____

_____

_____

_____

_____

_____

_____

_____

_____

_____

_____

_____

_____

_____

_____

_____

_____

_____

From driving a racecar through the Swiss Alps to recording
a massive pop hit, what are some things on your bucket list?

Maybe it didn't turn out perfectly, but it was worth it.
Whatever the outcome, what are some things
you're glad you tried?

_____

_____

_____

_____

_____

_____

_____

_____

_____

_____

_____

_____

_____

_____

_____

_____

_____

List your funniest memories!

_____

_____

_____

_____

_____

_____

_____

_____

_____

_____

_____

_____

_____

_____

_____

_____

_____

From that fancy restaurant your family goes to
on holidays to your local 24-hour diner,
what are your favorite places to eat?

_____

_____

_____

_____

_____

_____

_____

_____

_____

_____

_____

_____

_____

_____

_____

_____

_____

_____

Make a list of things nobody
knows about you.

Make a list of all the concerts you'd love to go to.

What are some things you like
to do by yourself?

_____

_____

_____

_____

_____

_____

_____

_____

_____

_____

_____

_____

_____

_____

_____

_____

From moonlight to your best friend's freckles,
list the most beautiful things you've ever seen.

Maybe you need to call Nana or your best friend from camp.
List all the people you ought to get in touch with!

_____
_____
_____
_____
_____
_____
_____
_____
_____
_____
_____
_____
_____
_____
_____
_____
_____

Glow-in-the-dark slime! Body scrubs! Egg terrariums!
List all of the DIY crafts you'd love to try.

_____

_____

_____

_____

_____

_____

_____

_____

_____

_____

_____

_____

_____

_____

_____

_____

_____

_____

_____

List times in your life where you felt truly independent.

From stingrays to turtles to anemones,
list your favorite sea creatures.

_____

_____

_____

_____

_____

_____

_____

_____

_____

_____

_____

_____

_____

_____

_____

_____

_____

_____

Maybe it's that one pop star or the vlogger
who makes you cringe with those awful jokes . . .
list celebrities you think are overrated.

_____

_____

_____

_____

_____

_____

_____

_____

_____

_____

_____

_____

_____

_____

_____

_____

_____

_____

From egg beaters to relish forks to potato mashers,
list the weirdest kitchen tools you can.

?!

List as many types of bears
as you can in 30 seconds!

Mittens, fuzzy socks, hot cocoa . . .
list what helps you survive winter.

_____

_____

_____

_____

_____

_____

_____

_____

_____

_____

_____

_____

_____

_____

_____

_____

_____

_____

Secret parties? Scheming?
List what you imagine adults do in their free time.

_____

_____

_____

_____

_____

_____

_____

_____

_____

_____

_____

_____

_____

_____

_____

_____

_____

_____

_____

List movies you've always wanted to watch.

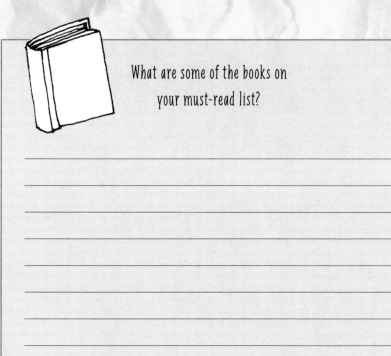

What are some of the books on
your must-read list?

Massive redwoods, brilliant zinnias, teeny clovers . . .
List your favorite plants.

From constellations to bioluminescence,
list natural phenomena that fill you with wonder.

_____

_____

_____

_____

_____

_____

_____

_____

_____

_____

_____

_____

_____

_____

_____

_____

_____

You've been given a crew and spaceship to explore the farthest reaches of our galaxy! Whether it's fluffy aliens or planets made of gemstone, what do you hope to discover on your travels?

_____

_____

_____

_____

_____

_____

_____

_____

_____

_____

_____

_____

_____

_____

_____

_____

_____

_____

_____

_____

Maybe you like pickle-and-peanut-butter sandwiches or licking rock salt. List weird foods you secretly enjoy.

_____

_____

_____

_____

_____

_____

_____

_____

_____

_____

_____

_____

_____

_____

_____

_____

From shoes that help you walk on walls to a headlamp
that reveals hidden lasers, list the tools you're bringing
on your secret spy mission.

What do you think your
pet thinks about?

_____

_____

_____

_____

_____

_____

_____

_____

_____

_____

_____

_____

_____

_____

_____

_____

_____

Write down all the important
birthdays you need to remember.

You're going on a road trip! From national parks
to roadside motels to famous fried food shacks, list all the sites
and experiences you're buckling up for.

WISH
YOU
WERE
HERE

Palmistry, tea-leaf reading, tarot cards . . .
how do you get in touch with your mystical side?

_____

_____

_____

_____

_____

_____

_____

_____

_____

_____

_____

_____

_____

_____

_____

_____

_____

_____

Listen, not everybody deserves an apple.
Rate your teachers from awesome to awful.

YAY!

Smart, giving, stubborn . . . List words you think your closest friends and family might use to describe you.

List fictional characters you'd
love to be friends with.

From fast-paced console adventures to retro
online role playing, list your favorite video games!

_____

_____

_____

_____

_____

_____

_____

_____

_____

_____

_____

_____

_____

_____

_____

Geography tests, fights with friends, doctor visits . . .
List things you worried about that turned out okay!

_____

_____

_____

_____

_____

_____

_____

_____

_____

_____

_____

_____

_____

_____

_____

_____

Hilarious, compassionate, lovable . . .
List some words you WANT people to use to describe you .

_____

_____

_____

_____

_____

_____

_____

_____

_____

_____

_____

_____

_____

_____

_____

_____

_____

_____

_____

From compatible senses of humor to a willingness to stand up for each other, list things you think are most important in a friendship.

List what you expect you'll be up
to when you're 25 years old.

List the best gifts you've ever gotten.

_____
_____
_____
_____
_____
_____
_____
_____
_____
_____
_____
_____
_____
_____
_____
_____
_____
_____
_____
_____
_____
_____

List the best gifts you've ever given.

Write down ridiculous stuff you've
overheard people say!

?!

From sharing their favorite jazz collection to hand-stitching you splendid Halloween costumes, what are the most special things that adults in your life have done for you?

Their smarts, their attitude, their clothes . . .
What makes older kids you admire so cool?

_____

_____

_____

_____

_____

_____

_____

_____

_____

_____

_____

_____

_____

_____

_____

_____

_____

_____

See a wild moose! Write a novel! Make homemade cinnamon buns!
List everything you want to do before your next birthday.

_____

_____

_____

_____

_____

_____

_____

_____

_____

_____

_____

_____

_____

_____

_____

_____

_____

_____

Fizzy, sugary, fruity . . . List different sodas
from delicious to disgusting.

_____

_____

_____

_____

_____

_____

_____

_____

_____

_____

_____

_____

_____

_____

_____

_____

From treasure hunter to dragon tamer,
what are some fantastical careers
you'd love to have?

They've got you covered when the going gets tough,
and they're always around for some good laughs.
List your squad.

_____

_____

_____

_____

_____

_____

_____

_____

_____

_____

_____

_____

_____

_____

From volcanoes to black holes, list things in
nature that kind of freak you out!

_____

_____

_____

_____

_____

_____

_____

_____

_____

_____

_____

_____

_____

_____

_____

_____

_____

_____

Maybe you hate sniffling and despise loud classmates.

List your pet peeves.

_____

_____

_____

_____

_____

_____

_____

_____

_____

_____

_____

_____

_____

_____

_____

Rank the apps you use,
from addictive to overrated.

_____

_____

_____

_____

_____

_____

_____

_____

_____

_____

_____

_____

_____

_____

_____

Sometimes life can feel a bit cinematic. From horse rides
through meadows to dancing in the rain,
list your life's movie moments so far!

_____

_____

_____

_____

_____

_____

_____

_____

_____

_____

_____

_____

_____

_____

_____

_____

_____

_____

From your burping talent to your impressive green thumb,
list things you want everybody to know about you.

List a bunch of nicknames you wish
people would call you.

HELLO
my name is

From jelly sandals to rainbow sweaters to striped socks,
list your favorite clothes in your closet!

_____

_____

_____

_____

_____

_____

_____

_____

_____

_____

_____

_____

_____

_____

_____

_____

_____

_____

_____

Perhaps you love chokers and despise lip gloss.
Rank accessories from essential to extra.

It happens to everyone from time to time...
List all the little white lies you've told.

_____
_____
_____
_____
_____
_____
_____
_____
_____
_____
_____
_____
_____
_____
_____
_____
_____
_____
_____
_____

List times you were SO hilarious
(even if other people didn't get it).

Maybe you love popping bubble wrap or
listening to waterfalls. List your favorite sounds.

From stomping around the house to a full-blown tantrum
in aisle 7 of the grocery store,
list your most memorable meltdowns.

_____

_____

_____

_____

_____

_____

_____

_____

_____

_____

_____

_____

_____

_____

_____

_____

_____

_____

_____

From hot showers to making dandelion wishes,
write a list of all the little things you find satisfying.

loves
me...

Loves
me not...

First best friend, first scary movie, first stinky cheese . . .
List big firsts you've had so far!

_____

_____

_____

_____

_____

_____

_____

_____

_____

_____

_____

_____

_____

_____

_____

_____

_____

_____

Whether you're crunching ice or pretending
your pillow is sentient, list the weirdest stuff you do.

?!

Remember that time you watched a pigeon eat a hotdog whole?
List the craziest stuff you've ever seen.

Choose something important to you and make
a list about why it should matter to everyone.

List some of the best compliments people have given you.

Comfy, loved, happy . . .
List some feelings you want to feel always.

You drank that unlabeled magic potion
and now you're immortal! Make a list of all the things
you're going to do with your never-ending story.

_____

_____

_____

_____

_____

_____

_____

_____

_____

_____

_____

_____

_____

_____

_____

_____

_____

_____

_____

_____

Friendship, a tropical hideaway, infinite list books . . .
List what you want more than anything!

_____

_____

_____

_____

_____

_____

_____

_____

_____

_____

_____

_____

_____

_____

_____

_____

Make a list of all the promises you've kept.

From that one mean kid in your class to kale chips,
list stuff you are so OVER.

List the best songs to have a good cry to.

Enticing snacks, unusual pets, different rules . . .
List the best parts of going to your friends' houses.

From climbing a tree to riding a motorbike, list things you haven't done yet!

Maybe you sit around wondering what the big deal
is with slime or what makes that boy band so dreamy.
List hype you don't get.

_____

_____

_____

_____

_____

_____

_____

_____

_____

_____

_____

_____

_____

_____

_____

_____

_____

From toy stores to clothing stores,
list your favorite places to shop!

List some mistakes you've made
that you forgive yourself for.

_____

_____

_____

_____

_____

_____

_____

_____

_____

_____

_____

_____

_____

_____

_____

_____

_____

_____

_____

_____

What do you think about before you fall asleep?
Make a list of the things that most often cross your mind
right before you drift off.

Charcoal-flavored ice cream, avocado lattes, mermaid toast . . .
List weird food trends you want to try!

_____

_____

_____

_____

_____

_____

_____

_____

_____

_____

_____

_____

_____

_____

_____

List times you've felt super lucky!

_____

_____

_____

_____

_____

_____

_____

_____

_____

_____

_____

_____

_____

_____

_____

_____

Nap time, riding in a stroller, mini juice boxes . . .
What were the best parts of being really little?

_____

_____

_____

_____

_____

_____

_____

_____

_____

_____

_____

_____

_____

_____

_____

_____

_____

_____

Maybe there will be hover-boards or robot pets.
List what you imagine the world will be like 25 years from now.

_____

_____

_____

_____

_____

_____

_____

_____

_____

_____

_____

_____

_____

_____

?!

List people you know whom you'd
love to become friends with.

Carefree, radiant, energized . . .
List all the ways sunshine makes you feel.

The dark can be spooky, but it can also be magical.
List all the things you feel at night.

Thunderstorms, hot tea, bonfires . . .
List things that help you get cozy.

List your favorite social media superstars.

Tax rebates? Laundry detergent?
List what you imagine adults talk about.

_____

_____

_____

_____

_____

_____

_____

_____

_____

_____

_____

_____

_____

_____

_____

_____

_____

If your moods were colors, what shades
would make up your rainbow today?

"I am funny, I am smart . . ."
List your "I"s!

_____

_____

_____

_____

_____

_____

_____

_____

_____

_____

_____

_____

_____

_____

_____

_____

_____

_____

_____

List qualities that you think
make somebody smart.

A pine tree, a river, a dragonfly . . .
List all the things you would be if you weren't human.

From family to passion to zeal,
list what is most important for a full life.

_____

_____

_____

_____

_____

_____

_____

_____

_____

_____

_____

_____

_____

_____

_____

_____

_____

_____

List names you're going to give your future pets.

_____

_____

_____

_____

_____

_____

_____

_____

_____

_____

_____

_____

_____

_____

_____

_____

_____

_____

_____

List the colors in order from favorite to least favorite
to design your own rainbow.

_____

_____

_____

_____

_____

_____

_____

_____

_____

_____

_____

_____

_____

_____

_____

_____

_____

_____

It's time to create some delicious sandwiches. Come up with
funny deli-style names and describe the ingredients you use.
They can be as zany as you want!

_____

_____

_____

_____

_____

_____

_____

_____

_____

_____

_____

_____

_____

_____

_____

_____

_____

Some days you want to dance, other days you need a good cry.
Whatever you're feeling today, list all the different emotions
you've experienced this week.

_____

_____

_____

_____

_____

_____

_____

_____

_____

_____

_____

_____

_____

_____

_____

_____

_____

_____

From movie nights to cookie-decorating to trips to the zoo,
list your favorite things to do with family.

_____

_____

_____

_____

_____

_____

_____

_____

_____

_____

_____

_____

_____

_____

_____

_____

_____

How are stars made? Why do humans have brains? What do sharks dream about? List some of your biggest questions about the universe.

Sometimes we all just want some PEACE and QUIET.
What do you do to relax? Go for a walk, read a book, snuggle up?
List your most soothing comforts.

_____

_____

_____

_____

_____

_____

_____

_____

_____

_____

_____

_____

_____

_____

_____

_____

Lemonade, coffee, veggie juice . . .
List your favorite beverages!

For your next trip to the moon, you've been asked to create a time capsule full of art, food, toys, and clothes representing the human species. Make a list of what you'd include.

_____

_____

_____

_____

_____

_____

_____

_____

_____

_____

_____

_____

_____

_____

_____

_____

_____

_____

_____

List as many stinky stenches as you
can think of in 30 seconds!

_____

_____

_____

_____

_____

_____

_____

_____

_____

_____

_____

_____

_____

_____

_____

_____

_____

_____

List all the things you're looking forward to doing this weekend.
Are you going to the movies, visiting a museum,
or playing outside with your friends?

_____

_____

_____

_____

_____

_____

_____

_____

_____

_____

_____

_____

_____

_____

_____

_____

_____

_____

What are some issues that you feel passionate about?
The environment? Politics? Animal rights? List them!

Maybe you'd like to be invisible, or fly, or both.

If you were a superhero what spectacular powers would you have?

_____

_____

_____

_____

_____

_____

_____

_____

_____

_____

_____

_____

_____

_____

Whether it's a tropical cruise or visiting Great-aunt Matilda in her rural summer home, rank all the trips you've been on from awesome to BORING.

Skipping rope, kickball, video games . . . What are some of your favorite ways to play with your friends? List them below.

_____

_____

_____

_____

_____

_____

_____

_____

_____

_____

_____

_____

_____

_____

_____

_____

_____

Sometimes art just isn't good! List the worst movies,
TV shows, and books you've ever endured.

_____

_____

_____

_____

_____

_____

_____

_____

_____

_____

_____

_____

_____

_____

_____

_____

_____

_____

Maybe you've traveled around the world,
or maybe you've never left your town. However
far you've gone, list your favorite places to be.

Bon Voyage

Not too long from now you'll be an adult. From getting your driver's license to buying your first house, what are some grownup activities you can't wait to do?

_____

_____

_____

_____

_____

_____

_____

_____

_____

_____

_____

_____

_____

_____

_____

_____

_____

From unicorns to hippogriffs to banshees,
list all the mythical creatures you wish existed.

Maybe you're thankful for your killer
electric guitar or your wonderful big brother.
List the things you're most grateful for.

_____

_____

_____

_____

_____

_____

_____

_____

_____

_____

_____

_____

_____

_____

_____

_____

Flan, jambalaya, filet mignon . . .
List some foods that you'd love to learn to cook.

_____

_____

_____

_____

_____

_____

_____

_____

_____

_____

_____

_____

_____

_____

_____

_____

_____

Your family has agreed to let you adopt any sort of pet you want!
What kooky animals would you love to have?

_____

_____

_____

_____

_____

_____

_____

_____

_____

_____

_____

_____

_____

_____

_____

_____

Who are your favorite artists? They can be writers, actors, musicians, or painters—whatever they make, celebrate them here!

List as many naturally blue plants
and animals as you can in 30 seconds!

_____

_____

_____

_____

_____

_____

_____

_____

_____

_____

_____

_____

_____

_____

_____

_____

Recess, math class, lunch . . . Make a list ranking parts
of the school day from best to worst.

There's nothing wrong with feeling sad sometimes,
but it's helpful to know what you can do to feel better.
Make a list of all the things that cheer you up.

Maybe you want to research the history of secret codes
or teach yourself how to make crunchy slime.
What do you want to learn more about?

_____

_____

_____

_____

_____

_____

_____

_____

_____

_____

_____

_____

_____

_____

_____

_____

_____

_____

You've won the lottery! You're now the richest person in the whole world. Maybe you'll donate to charity or buy a lifetime supply of banana candy. Whatever you'd do, list it!

Summer is the best. School's out, and so is the sun.
Whether you're running a lemonade stand or relaxing with friends,
make a list of the best parts of summer.

_____

_____

_____

_____

_____

_____

_____

_____

_____

_____

_____

_____

_____

_____

_____

_____

_____

Maybe you said sorry even though you didn't want to,
or conquered stage fright to dance in the school play.
List moments when you've felt really proud of yourself.

_____

_____

_____

_____

_____

_____

_____

_____

_____

_____

_____

_____

_____

_____

_____

_____

_____

_____

_____

_____

_____

Your aptitude with animals, your contagious laugh, your curiosity . . .
What are some things that make YOU quintessentially YOU?